C000068905

The 7 C's of Success

C'ing is Doing & Doing is Seeing

by

Shaun T. Benjamin

WingSpan Press

© copyright 2010 Shaun T. Benjamin

If this book does not have a cover, it may be stolen property. Stripped
books do not tally payments for the publisher or the author.

This book is a work of nonfiction. Any resemblance to actual events,
people or locales is entirely coincidental. Named references have
been changed intentionally to maintain confidentiality.

Visit the Web Site:
www.ShauntBenjamin.com and/or www.ShauntBejanian.com

All Rights Reserved, including the right of reproduction
in whole or in part in any form.

Printed in the United States of America

Published by WingSpan Press, Livermore, CA
www.wingspanpress.com

The WingSpan name, logo and colophon are the trademarks of
WingSpan Publishing.

Design by PANGEA Corporation
Second Edition 2015

ISBN: 978-1-59594-566-2
Library of Congress Control Number: 2010923733

THE 7 C's OF SUCCESS
TABLE OF CONTENTS

ACKNOWLEDGEMENT

This book is dedicated to my lovely children Mike (Vrej, 19) and Melo (Melody, 13), my conscience and core of creation, who have taught me unconditional love and gratitude, and to my beautiful wife Vera who has whole-heartedly supported me in every endeavor and has taught me to be sympathetic and nonjudgmental. I feel blessed and I am eternally grateful. I thank God, the source of all my inspiration and creation, for providing me with the idea and the insight to write this book. I am indebted to my parents (Sam and Nora) for teaching me about faith and for their love and dedication to fulfill our needs when needed. I am forever grateful to my brother Shawn, his wife Donna and their talented children Joan-Seda and Michael for their love and support. I am grateful to my brother Shawn who has always believed in me regardless of what I have undertaken and for being there 24/7 to support and encourage and offer unlimited ideas and advice. I am indebted to to my oldest sister Seda, who has a heart of gold along with her husband Joseph and their amazing children Allen, Armen and Alina. I am grateful for having my younger sister Anjell in my life for providing me with such powerful support from three thousand miles away that penetrates deep into the soul. I am dwarfed by her humanity, intelligence, generosity and sound advice. I am grateful to my dear friend Hellen Petrosyan and her amazing daughter Eline Rachel for their heart-felt prayers and for always being there through hard times. They are truly God's angels. Special thanks for all my benevolent mentors, Martin Landau, Mark Rydell, Lyle Kessler, the late Susan Peretz and Allan Miller, all from The Actors Studio who have contributed immensely to my artistic life.

My gratitude to one of my special martial arts masters Tom Callos, whose passion to give and promote kindness, has been an example to follow. I am much obliged to Master Callos for his incessant support and encouragement. I thank Judy Kellem for her input and kind remarks. I thank Jared Ali for everything he has taught me. I thank my dear friend Tamas Menyhart for his amazing faith and belief. I am grateful to Peter Lupus III and Gene Mitchell, my special brothers from other mothers, for their special friendship. "Gene, you've been an inspiration to me through my entire artistic life and I am eternally grateful." I thank Mr. Peter Lupus for his constant belief and encouragement, and for being an epitome of kindness and respect. To all my students at Shaun T Benjamin Karate, who are a bastion of love, support and inspiration, thank you for sharing your triumphs with us! Special thanks to Mr. Arno Yesayan, truly a LIONHEART for saving my life when I was down and out. "Mr. Arno, you are the epitome of humanity and humility and everything that H.I.G.H. K.E.Y. F.I.T.N.E.S.S. stands for. You are truly an angel from God and I am blessed to have you in my life. You are indeed Faith in action and the world needs more people like you. THANK YOU."

I would like to thank Mr. David Collins for giving me an opportunity to get this book published. Without him, this would have been impossible and I am so grateful.

Last but not least, I would like to thank my dear friend and editor John Schulte, his wife Cheryl Ann Wong, their beautiful daughter Blythe Abigail and their partner John Charles Besmehn from PANGEA. I cannot possibly thank John Schulte enough for his dedication, suggestions, hard work, support, patience, belief and encouragement. His passion and his extraordinary compassion are phenomenal. "John, you are indeed a man of stupendous integrity. You are meticulous and conscientious and a man of your word. I will never forget how you stayed up so late on New Year's Eve with your daughter sick with chicken pox and finished editing the book because you said you would. I have learned so much from you about honesty, integrity, honor and humility. Your humanity and generosity surpasses all understanding. Thank you my dearest friend."

ABOUT SHAUN T BENJAMIN

Shaun T Benjamin, a sixth degree martial arts master and a lifetime member of The Actors Studio, is the President and CEO of Melody Films Entertainment Inc., a company dedicated to producing life-affirming films and TV shows with positive, inspirational messages. He has been recognized by Cambridge *Who's Who* for demonstrating dedication, contribution, leadership and excellence in coaching, acting, writing, directing, producing, human transformation and inspirational film production.

Prompted by a desire to inspire and raise consciousness regarding the unstoppable human spirit, the power within, Mr. Benjamin established a film production outfit in 2002, in order to make movies that inspire and heal people. A firm believer that "Martial Arts" and "Acting" are vehicles for self-transformation, he has recently written, and will direct and produce a film, *A Fighting Chance*, an inspirational family sports drama, which tells the story of a father who teaches his young son and daughter how to tap into their own internal powers to overcome obstacles. It is about Faith overcoming Fear. Shaun will star in the film with his son Mike Coleman, his daughter Melody Angel and the Academy Award Winner, Hollywood Acting legend, Martin Landau.

Mr. Benjamin is also the Creator/Founder of the *High Key Fitness Karate* system, an international sport karate curriculum that teaches self-enhancement, self-discipline, respect, positive attitude and self-discovery through the use of the Martial Arts. This system is currently being introduced to high schools and colleges as a tool to empower the students to realize their God-given potential to make a positive impact and contribute to the world. Having been a world champion himself, Shaun has trained a number of National and World sport karate champions.

Mr. Benjamin is also the Creator of the international *Nothing But the Truth Acting* system (Divine8Acting) which teaches everyone with a desire how to be a great actor. This system is also being introduced to high schools and colleges around the world. He is currently writing his next movie, *Acting Crazy*, a family drama about the complex Hollywood system, faith and reaching one's dreams.

Mr. Benjamin attributes his humble success in multiple disciplines to his faith in God, guidance of his mentors, his students, his parents and siblings, and the incessant support and love he receives from his wife Vera and his children Mike and Melody.

Shaun holds a BSEE degree from Northeastern University, Boston, certificate courses in Filmmaking and Writing from UCLA Extension, Acting//Directing credentials at The Actors Studio (Mentors: Martin Landau, Mark Rydell) and an MSQA from CSUDH. Mr. Benjamin lives in Glendale, California with his family and looks forward to continuing to make a difference as an actor, writer, director, teacher and a film producer. Shaun also teaches seminars as a "Life Coach" and helps people discover their Purpose and create a "Blueprint" for its accomplishment to have a fulfilling life.

www.melodyfilmsentertainment.com
www.shauntbenjamin.com
www.shauntbejanian.com
www.shauntbenjaminkarate.com
www.7csofsuccess.com

FOREWORD

By Peter Lupus

I am proud to be a close friend of Shaun T Benjamin. I have known him for over twenty years, and in all this time, he has always had clear goals set before him — and with great discipline, tireless effort and self-sacrifice, he has always accomplished those goals. Amazingly, while in pursuit of his own targeted aspirations, he has always found time and energy to help many others to reach their goals.

I met Shaun through my son Peter III, and from the very first meeting, I knew why Peter introduced him as "my very good friend." Shaun has had a wonderful influence on my son over the years and, from what I have heard and seen, Peter has been a great friend to Shaun.

I urge you to read Shaun's book with great care. As you do, you will realize why my wife, Sharon, and I consider Shaun as our other son, and Peter III considers Shaun as the brother he never had. This is a book of wonderful insight and depth, written, distilled and filtered for everyone to understand. The thoughts are complex, but the messages are conveyed with beautiful simplicity.

This outstanding book expresses the life of Shaun T Benjamin, his discipline, his high morals, his strong belief in the love of our Father in heaven, and the deep desire to help all those with whom he comes in contact. Not once have I known Shaun to put his success before the success of others. This is a great aspect of his character and strength. When you read this book, you will know, as we all know, and love Shaun, that the only way Shaun T Benjamin spells success is L-O-V-E.

I'm sure, like me, you won't be able to read this book without reappraising yourself and finding some more ways to be a more helpful all around friend to those you associate with and to those you hold dear.

Shaun, I pray your life-long companions will continue to be good health, happiness, prosperity, charity and love.

Your lifelong friend,

Peter Lupus

About Peter Lupus

S tar of the original *Mission Impossible* TV series, Peter Lupus portrayed Willie Armitage, the force's muscle man. At 6' 4" tall, while developing his amazing physique and strength, Peter earned the bodybuilding titles of Mr. Indianapolis, Mr. Indiana, Mr. Hercules and Mr. International Health Physique. After *Mission Impossible*, Peter went on to star in sundry television shows, including *Fantasy Island, Love Boat* and *Police Squad!* He has also executive produced the film *Curse of the Forty-Niner*. A testament to his own tenacity and amazing achievements as a world-class bodybuilder, Mr. Lupus is the holder of the world record in lifting a total of 77,185 lbs in 26 minutes and 50 seconds at the age of 75! His next attempt will be on his 80th birthday, June 2012.

Mr. Lupus is also a successful entrepreneur. He is currently the chairman of Revolucion World Wide, a company that distributes natural whole food drinks and products through the direct sales approach. This company and its natural products are what Peter's entire life has been about – good nutrition, regular exercise, and a strong faith.

INTRODUCTION

A s a "Martial Arts" Master Instructor and an "Acting" coach, I have often been asked "how" to achieve a desired goal. There are many different ways of going about it and I am positive a variety of books have been written that have some great methods to offer.

Having inspired, advised, instructed and guided students for the last thirty years, my contribution to the answer of how to attain your goals is the following simple, yet solid seven-step-method, provided in an easily understandable everyday language.

The fact that you do have a desire, a goal, a "want" or a dream is to be admired, acknowledged and encouraged. Surprisingly, it is not easy to know what you want.

Unfortunately, many people feel they live a mundane existence and despite the fact that they may know what they want, they still struggle with finding and implementing a simple and reasonable method to achieve their dreams. They are simply unable to know how to go about getting their heart's desire.

Only a small percentage of people (approximately 4%) know exactly what they want and how to go about getting it. Those few people also know where they are going and actually know that they will get there with utmost certainty.

If you are reading this book, you are seeking to find an answer to set you on the right path. I believe with absolute confidence that you will find the answer in this book and by utilizing it methodically, with diligence and persistent effort, you will be amongst the top achievers and you will reach your goals and dreams.

I remember years ago I was scheduled to have a counseling

session with Maggie, a fifty-year-old mother of one of my Karate students, who was seeking my advice about a personal dilemma. I had seen Maggie a few times when she would drop off her 12-year-old son, Paul, for his Karate lessons. She seemed extremely authoritative and controlling and critical of Paul, which had contributed to his low self-esteem and self-consciousness.

When she showed up at my office for her appointment, after exchanging niceties, she burst out crying right away. She could not control her emotions. It was obvious she was in desperate need of some help. I listened to her pour her heart out for half an hour about how horrible life had been since her husband had left her two years ago. She was under the impression that everything that was happening to her was a bad omen and there were people out there who were trying to stop her from succeeding. Needless to say, Maggie was distressed and despondent, and her main focus and concentration throughout the day was that her life was getting worse and worse and her health was deteriorating. She was also seeking help from a psychiatrist who had prescribed her some medicine for depression that was affecting her mood.

Maggie thought she had no control over her life or her future. She had no idea that she was the one who was causing all of her problems through negative thinking and by surrounding herself with people who were full of fear and superstition. Her so-called friends spent much of their time circulating mean-spirited gossip.

Primarily, Maggie was wallowing in self-pity and she wanted me to commiserate with her self-indulgence. I refused to participate in her pity-party and she was taken aback when I broke her pattern by staying silent until she finished wailing. I asked her calmly, "Are you finished crying yet?" She was insulted by my direct and unsympathetic inquiry. This might sound callous to somebody who does not know me. I am extremely sensitive and I care for people. I felt her pain and I knew if I had joined in and sympathized with her, it would not have changed her situation. As a matter of fact, it would have exacerbated it. I knew I had to be strong and I had to impart some information that she might not have wanted to hear, yet it was the truth and it would set her free. I said, "Maggie, you have created everything you are experiencing right now. No one else is responsible but you. You are creating it right now as you are speaking negatively about your circumstances. You shape your own destiny." She looked at me as if I had grown a second head and she was perturbed by the fact that I had put it all back on her shoulders. I had to go all the way with this, so I continued. "Remember sweetheart, today is yesterday's tomorrow. In other words, your experience today is a result of what you've thought about, said and concentrated on yesterday." I noticed a look of concern on her face so I consoled her right away. "Despite all of what I've said, the good news is you can change all of that right now. You can change the course of your life this very instant. Regardless of how long you've been in negativity, by thinking and saying positive life-affirming words with a solid conviction behind them, you can change your current unwanted set of circumstances. You can change them by changing the words that come out of your mouth. Your belief in what you say is what makes it so."

Maggie then asked, "How do I stop myself from thinking negatively when the people I see on a daily basis are all confirming what I think?" She did not like the answer I gave her but I had to be honest. "Maggie, you have to stay away from people who are negative because faith comes by hearing. You develop either a positive faith or a negative faith depending on what you hear. Anything you give your attention to magnifies and eventually becomes a recurring thought or a dominant thought. Ultimately, your dominant thought becomes your reality, your truth or your belief. And when you believe something with all your heart and soul, positive or negative, you experience it in your life because of your actions. There is no way around it. This is a universal law that operates with mathematical accuracy. Whatever you focus on and believe internally, therefore, will materialize externally in your physical world.

Anything internalized, will be externalized.
Whatever is impressed by the mind, will be expressed by real experience in the physical world.

"That is how important it is, Maggie, for you to be extremely cautious about what you say and what you think. Every time you are tempted to open your mouth to express something negative, become aware of the impact, then change your thought and express the opposite. Say something positive. Why choose the negative when the positive is just as easily accessible? You always act on your belief whether you realize it or not. Why not create the things you want and not the things you don't want?"

Maggie just sat there and listened attentively and tried to absorb as much as she could. I also wanted to take advantage of the fact that she was in a receptive mode to bring up her son Paul's situation. I knew if she continued talking to him the way she did, Paul was going to have a very tough, possibly ruined-life. The poor kid was shy, self conscious and unsure of himself. He had been criticized to such an extent that he never believed in himself, never thought he could do anything right. He had slowly become what his mother had called him to be: "inadequate," "sloppy," "awkward," "lazy," "shy," and "stupid." I finally mustered up the courage to tell her the truth about Paul. "Maggie, I'm sorry to drop the ball on you all at once, but the fact that your son Paul is shy and emotionally unexpressive is because you created him that way. He can't do anything right around you. You are always critical of everything he does. He is afraid of you because all he hears from you is harsh criticism. He has become what you have called him to be. He is your creation. You made him believe everything you labeled him by constant criticism; he became what he believed and felt to be true about himself.

"Is it any wonder that children who are unsociable and lack self-confidence have constantly been criticized by parents, teachers, peers and relatives? That is why so many people (young and old) suffer from lack of self-esteem." I noticed Maggie getting emotional again. Tears were rolling down her cheeks but this time she was not hysterical. It was genuine hurt emanating from the core of her being. Deeply touched, I could barely contain my own emotion and continued, "On the contrary, children who are confident, sociable and naturally expressive are the children who are constantly inspired, supported, encouraged and loved by their parents and their immediate surroundings."

Maggie sat in my office quietly for a few more minutes. A genuine serenity had overtaken her body that made her humble and peaceful. She was grateful for this new insight. Maggie left my office with a resolve to take good care of Paul and stop hanging around negative people.

I saw her throw her arms around Paul who had just finished class and kiss him on the cheek. Paul's awkward and nervous reaction to this unexpected loving gesture brought tears to my eyes. Paul hugged his mother tightly and they walked out of the studio. I knew right then and there that Maggie and Paul were going to be all right.

Beware:
Your words create your world and
ultimately your children's world!

AUTHOR'S NOTE

In the following seven chapters, I introduce and explain the 7 C's of "success." "Success" means different things to different people; however, in this book, it means being Physically, Mentally, Spiritually (Emotionally) and Financially prosperous. "Success" is having: Happiness, Health, Wealth, Joy, Security, Peace of mind, Comfort and a kind, generous and forgiving pure heart.

At the end of this book, there are powerful verses and affirmations that can be used to overcome negative thinking – whether it comes from within yourself – or someone contaminates your dreams and visions, you can arrest the negative thoughts with these accessible motivational messages to keep you focused and in good spirit.

THE 1ST C OF SUCCESS

COMMITMENT

Set a goal and pledge to stay faithful.

CHAPTER 1.

COMMITMENT

Once you decide on a goal, you commit to it whole-heartedly. This is where your integrity becomes an important issue in keeping your commitment. You pledge allegiance to your desire that you will not steer away from your purpose.

When you stay loyal to your commitment, you build a solid reputation for doing what you said you would do. Your integrity stays intact with you and with those around you — and people can count on you and believe you and trust you with a project or any other assignment.

When you do not honor your own pledge, your word does not weigh much with people who know you; they cannot count on you, so you lose credibility. Your commitment does not mean anything to you or to others. You do not even believe in what you say, so how can others be expected to believe in you? We are all familiar with the statement "He's all talk, but no action." This is a bad reputation to have.

Our words are powerful and they truly create our worlds. People know us by how faithful we are to our promises. If you have said you would do something, you have got to understand that it is a promise, an oath, a pledge etched in stone that no matter what, you will follow through because you said you would. You have got to do your ultimate best, everything in your power, to bring your promises to fruition.

School is a commitment.

Marriage is a commitment.

Getting a degree is a commitment.

Supporting someone is a commitment.

Getting a black belt is a commitment.

Working towards and attaining your goals — this is the meaning of "commitment." You cannot just haphazardly exonerate yourself from this responsibility because you are having a bad day and you do not feel like doing it now, or because you are experiencing obstacles along the way. You must plough through with the courage of your commitment and take action and be consistent, which is the topic of our next chapter.

THE 2ND C OF SUCCESS

CONSISTENCY

Discipline yourself to take action daily.

CHAPTER 2.

CONSISTENCY

Consistency is the ability to self-discipline and do a certain thing at a certain time at certain intervals, regardless of any unexpected hurdles. It means you are tenacious and persistent about achieving your goal and you steadfastly persevere to adhere to your set of principles, whatever values or standards you may have set for yourself. Nothing can stop you from going forward.

Imagine you want to be a great piano player, a great Martial Artist, a scientist or a professional basketball player — and you only spend a couple of hours a week practicing; and sometimes when your cousin Larry shows up, you miss your classes because you have to spend time with him. Do you really expect to get what you want with this kind of consistency? Your goal must be literally holy — and it should mean everything to you. Shooting the breeze with Larry, for the sake of being polite or whatever, is not going to bring you closer to your goal.

Do not sacrifice your goal for anything or anyone.

You have been given a gift of unlimited potential to do anything! You can become who you want to be. Are you going to let that go to waste?

It is your choice.

The secret to succeeding in any endeavor is doing things consistently, on a daily basis, in small gradual increments. These small but consistent, incremental actions increase the certainty of attaining your desired goal. Each day being one step closer to your dream takes you closer to its reality and solidity. And each step should also increase the power within you to achieve your goal – because it is that much closer to becoming a physical reality. Consistency, then, is a key tool to turn your dreams into realities! This is the hardest thing for people to understand because most people look at the big picture and they get scared, overwhelmed and discouraged. As a result, they take no action thinking that it will not matter anyway, so they give up on their dreams.

What do you want?

What is your purpose in life?

What are you fighting for?

What do you really want?

Who are you fighting for?

What are you trying to do?

What is at stake for you?

What do you live for?

Who do you live for?

What moves you?

What are you passionate about?

What does your heart tell you?

Where are you going?

Do you see yourself there?

Are you willing to do what it takes to get there?

How badly do you want it?

Why do you want it?

Find your "why."

Become clear about what it is that you want and then make a commitment and take consistent action on a daily basis to bring yourself closer to your goal.

What kind of standards have you set for yourself and are you consistent in maintaining and fulfilling those standards?

Be honest with yourself. This is for you and nobody else. You are not out there trying to prove something to anybody. You are just trying to be the best you can be at whatever you pursue, and operate at your maximum God-given potential.

I believe the first two steps are clear: make a decision about what you want, make a commitment to that desire and take action consistently with confidence to get yourself closer to your goal. CONFIDENCE is the topic of our next chapter.

You should be feeling how this system is all building and linking together. By the time you have completed this book, you will understand the inter-related nature of the 7 C's and how important it is to harness each of these powers to attain your dreams.

THE 3RD C OF SUCCESS

CONFIDENCE

Believe because you are backed by faith.

CHAPTER 3.

CONFIDENCE

Confidence is the most important and crucial step in accomplishing your desired goal. The understanding and execution of this step will catapult you into solidifying the realization of your dream. The lack of its execution, however, can break you and leave you disappointed. So, please pay attention!

Confidence is "belief" in one's own abilities backed and supported by a firm "trust" and "faith" in a "Higher Being." It is an "inner knowing" that is undeniable and unstoppable. A confident person possesses a firm "conviction" with "indomitable spirit" that no one or no-thing can or will get in the way of getting what is wanted. Confident people are "bold" and "courageous" in the face of obstacles. They do not take "no" for an answer because they "know" they are backed by the most amazing power in the world which is omnipresent, omnipotent and omniscient.

Having confidence means having faith in one's own abilities and God-given gifts. It counts for nothing, however, if you don't "do" anything with your gifts. You cannot just sit somewhere and claim you have faith and do nothing.

"Faith is acting on what you believe."

I strongly believe this is a great definition of faith. Some people think "faith" is a religious term and they ignore the true meaning of it, not knowing that it is the most important ingredient for success in any chosen field.

Developing positive effective faith has everything to do with your "inner belief" and has nothing to do with your creed, your gender, the color of your skin, your geographical location, your ethnicity, your national origin, your occupation or your social status.

If you have faith, you have confidence -- that "firm belief" in yourself and your abilities, all backed by a higher power to create anything in your life. It is that "inner knowing" deep down inside of you, which tells you that you are unstoppable in the face of obstacles. Confident people have an indomitable spirit that guides them through every negative situation with grace and a positive attitude. The words "defeat," "impossible," "no," or "can't" do not exist in their vocabulary. On the contrary, they consider every setback a victory because it brings them one step closer to their goal.

The Bible says: "Faith without action is dead."

Now read it backwards:

"Dead is action without faith."

This statement means a lot to me because no matter which way you read it, you need both "action" and "faith" to succeed. As you can see, "action" and "faith" are so intertwined such that you can even read the phrase backwards and it has equal power. Your faith means nothing if you do not take action and your action means nothing if you do not have faith. Faith is not passive; it is active, living – it is a force!

Imagine for a minute if you will, regardless of the obstacles, the actions you would take and the things you would do if you truly believed that there was no way you could fail. True faith is when there is absolutely no doubt in your mind that you are going to get to your destination. That is true confidence: believing and knowing the absolute attainment of your future goal now as if you already have it.

The old adage, "seeing is believing" only makes sense if it alludes to seeing with your mind's eye (visualizing). On the contrary, if the phrase alludes to actually physically seeing something now, it does not make spiritual sense at all. It is like saying, "I want proof before I can believe. I've got to see God before I believe in Him."

Spiritually speaking, it is exactly the opposite that is true. True faith states:

"Believing is seeing."

You have got to believe (now) before you can see (later) the physical evidence.

The Bible in Hebrews 11:1 states: "Now faith is the substance of things hoped for, the evidence of things not seen."

In this verse "hoped for" (in Archaic English) means confidence. It is the feeling that what is wanted will be had. You have the blueprint crystallized in your mind as truth. You have believed and received your desire as true in the spiritual realm. Now you have to take action and bring it to physical fruition.

Confident people believe in their inevitable success one hundred percent and they take action now. One can remember the concept here by thinking of N.O.W. as an acronym (No Obstacles Whatsoever). They never allow any negativity to enter their minds.

Please pay attention. This is one of the most important truths you will ever need to know. I have also expressed it through the ease of acronyms.

F.A.I.T.H. = Follow Action In The Heart

N.O.W. = No Obstacles Whatsoever

f.a.i.t.h n.o.w. or n.o.w. f.a.i.t.h.

Faith is taking action now!

You must never give up on your goal.

You keep going, regardless of the obstacles, until you attain your desire.

The Bible in 1 Timothy 6:12 states: "fight the good fight of faith."

It is a good fight because you always win.

You just keep fighting until you win.

Belief + Action = Faith

The notion of "fighting" in the above verse means keeping the focus and never losing sight of one's desired goal -- the crystallized picture in your mind. It means keeping your eyes on the prize and never diverting or getting veered off by distractions and temptations. You only have one possibility: the victorious possibility!

This is a good place for me to give you an example of what I am talking about.

An extraordinary black belt Master instructor, Mr. Arno Yesayan, an epitome of character, leadership and humility, participated in the world championship sport karate competition in Las Vegas a few years ago.

As soon as the competition started, Mr. Arno received an illegal kick to the groin during his first fight that left him incapacitated for a few minutes. The excruciating pain would have made anyone give up. The judges asked him to forfeit the match to avoid any further damage.

Mr. Arno knew, however, that he had already seen and believed the victory in his mind the night before. He had already won the fight before he got into the ring. He had seen himself clearly holding up the world championship trophy. Mr. Arno could not accept what was happening to him at the time and did not believe his physical senses. He knew he had to fight the good fight of faith and he knew he would win. He just had to stand up and carry through the physical action.

What he was seeing with his physical eyes did not match with what he had seen with his eyes of faith the night before and years ago when he had set the goal. Mr. Arno mustered up the courage to stand up and carry through his vision and he won all his fights in his weight division and stood there victorious, holding up the world championship trophy exactly the way he had envisioned it. Mr. Arno, truly an amazing human being, is a great example for my children and all our students and I feel honored to have him in our lives. He defines what courage, faith, confidence and humility is all about.

My students constantly inspire me and I always learn from them. I am eternally grateful for their contribution to my life.

Faith is the positive expectancy of a victorious outcome.

f.a.i.t.h. n.o.w. $\rightarrow$ physical manifestation later.

The important fact to remember here is that, as I mentioned before, you have to be careful who you hang around with and who you listen to because it will affect your faith one way or another. Remember: faith comes by hearing. You can develop a positive faith or a negative faith depending on what you hear. Be careful with whom you share your dreams because one deliberate or unintentional comment can destroy everything for which you have worked. Protect your vision. Guard your spirit.

What you believe becomes your truth. What do you want to believe? Negativity, Lack, Pessimism, Gossip, Backbiting and Sarcasm, all of which lead to self-sabotage? Or do you want to believe in Joy, Peace, Optimism, Appreciation, Gratitude, Positive Mental Attitude, Love and Kindness, which all lead to peace, success and prosperity?

What constitutes your truth? What are your set of beliefs and characteristics that make you who you are? That is the topic in our next step, number four: CHARACTER.

However, before we go to the next step, I would like to bring up an important example that illustrates the application of all three steps so far.

Let's say that, for instance, you have decided to improve your physical appearance and release thirty pounds and get down to your ideal weight. You must first write it down and commit yourself to this goal. However, you have to be cautious about how you phrase your intention. If you write down for example, "I want to lose 30 pounds." you are going to have a problem right off the bat for three obvious reasons.

Firstly, when you lose something, your body, which has a tendency to look for what it has lost, may find the weight and put it back on! Sooner or later you are going to put that weight back on without realizing that you are subconsciously being driven toward your written statement. Your body will not rest until it puts that weight back on because something is missing. That is precisely why so many people who are on a particular diet do well for a while and then they go back to their old habits where they feel comfortable.

Second reason why people are unable to accomplish the aforementioned goal is because they do not see immediate results, so they give up. They are seeking instant gratification. They are not careful about what they say about themselves. They constantly criticize the shape of their own bodies; they complain about how hard it is to lose weight. But remember: if your thoughts, spoken words and actions do not line up with your desire, then you are going to find it very difficult to get back into shape and you will eventually get frustrated, discouraged and give up.

It is imperative that you grasp the fact that whatever destination (predominant thought) your mind is focused on, your body is going there now. If you criticize the excessive fat on your body and condemn it, guess what -- you are going to get more of it because that is your governing thought. I know this sounds strange, but it is true. Fix your attention (focus) on your intention (victorious final image) and reject any other ideas contrary to that.

Thirdly, if you have not already done it in your mind, you cannot do it in the body. In other words, you have to see the final picture in your mind and lock in the victorious outcome before you get started. You must believe it before you see it; or you must see it in your mind's eye before you see the physical evidence. This is where Confidence and Faith come into play. There should be no doubt in your mind that you can do this and no one or nothing can stop you. You must believe whole-heartedly that you have already achieved this victory. That is why this step is extremely crucial.

I always advise my Karate students the night before a major competition to imagine five opponents of different shapes and sizes. I tell them to visualize beating those opponents in their minds, one at a time, and then really feel the victorious outcome and see themselves getting first place trophies. They know they have to win the match in their minds before they enter the ring. They enter the ring knowing they have already won. The result is 100% successful when the students do this exercise diligently the night before. The reason is -- if you have won it in your mind, your body will follow suit. But you must realize that you still have to get out there and physically do it. Nothing happens without action.

I also advise my acting students to do the same. I ask them to work really hard and prepare the best way they know how for an audition. I ask them to visualize themselves impressing everyone in the room and then see themselves working on the set and finally visualize watching the show on television with their loved ones and imagine receiving all the happy phone calls from well-wishers, friends and relatives from all over the world.

Going back to our example, here is the kind of statement one could use to meditate and visualize:

"I, [your name], eat a healthy diet and exercise regularly. I know I look great at my desired weight of --- pounds. I feel happy and joyful for the entire day when I exercise. I am in perfect physical health and perfect physical shape. I weigh --- pounds, have a -- inch waist," et cetera....

Now your mind focuses on "healthy diet," "perfect shape,"

"perfect health," "perfect weight," et cetera.... And you are subconsciously driven towards your target weight. Your actions, therefore, will consistently match your predominant thought and ultimately you will fulfill your commitment.

However, one must realize that action needs to be taken. Without action, your mental picture will ultimately die.

A student once asked me why he lost a tournament. He had pre-determined that he was the victor. His vision, he said, was clear and there were no obstacles in his way. He had also done the physical work. He had solid faith and conviction that when the competition was over, he would be receiving top honors. He imagined himself claiming the trophy and accepting congratulations from his peers and family. He lost his final match unfortunately and took second place on that day.

"Why, Master, did I lose?" he said. I looked my student in the eyes. I could see his intensity. It was not easy for me to tell him, but I had to make him aware of what he was up against.

"I know the student you were fighting against who won," I said. "He is obviously very capable. But he is not a better fighter than you. He won because he had a stronger and clearer vision than you. He was more determined, more assured, more decided. In other words, he had stronger faith, without an ounce of doubt in his mind that he was going to be the winner today and he took action on his belief and fought hard. If you were to fight him again and if you prepare yourself more mentally, you will win. I know what he is capable of – and I know what your strengths are, too. He beat you because his mind was more focused. You are a stronger fighter, but you lost to him on the mat because you were not mentally as strong; you were slightly hesitant. You must know without a hint of doubt that you are the victor and lock in your victorious picture -- do not waiver and act on your belief. You must enter the ring with total confidence. " My student learned humility that day!

The next tournament came along and my student was matched up again with his great opposition. This time he psyched himself up as I have never before seen. He went into the competition on fire. He was ablaze with desire. Even I could see him clearly now, standing with the trophy in his hands. I nodded to him assuredly as he went in for the bout. I knew then that my student was going to win. And he did. "Master," he said. "You are right. The last time I saw myself winning, but I also saw flashes of my opponent winning. I was too concerned about him winning and I trained with a slight doubt in the back of my mind. This time, I locked in the winning picture and trained hard with confidence and total faith. I carried that into the ring and acted on my belief knowing ahead of time that I was going to come out victorious. This time, it was just me. I knew it and I felt it before it ever happened." There is no doubt when you possess total conviction. ACTION with FAITH or FAITH with ACTION makes it all happen. One without the other is powerless and it will fall short.

This is a good place for me to address something that has been on my mind for a long time. I do not like to criticize others and I advise people against it; however, I believe this is very important because it has to do with awareness.

The book and the DVD The Secret by Rhonda Byrne has misguided and misinformed many people about the process of creation and has presented the information in a simple way as if no one needs to take any action. Another thing emphasized in The Secret is gaining material things without any spiritual stipulation. The so-called principle, "the law of attraction," a pseudo-scientific term, is referenced throughout the book and DVD. The DVD talks about the creative process in three distinct steps, Ask, Believe and Receive, as if one is done after the other on three separate occasions. The message in The Secret has confused a lot of people. I see that many people have been distracted by it and have only achieved marginal success using the techniques. Perhaps because many noted self-help celebrities endorsed the work (many of whom were paid to appear in the documentary), it was met with great fanfare in 2005. But I call the work's message "the law of distraction" since so many people were distracted from the truth of life and believed that this is a trick they can learn to use to gain material things. The message has been reduced to: if you visualize, you materialize.

It is not that simple. There are so many steps involved in going from visualization to materialization that has not been explained. If it were that easy, everyone would be doing it and everyone would have what they wanted. I also have noticed that since The Secret so many people have become greedy and have tried to get "stuff" by either overcharging, or deceiving or developing a "get-get" mentality.

Many have tried to market what little they know about anything without the consumer in mind. Many have tried to open a half-hearted business with half-hearted service, thinking that they are going to become rich if they visualize people coming to them.

They have completely forgotten about serving the client; honestly, the intent should be to offer a service that benefits others. These temporary and superficial believers have gained marginal success and have attributed their success to using the so-called "secret." And then somehow they lose money or they lose their business or the money comes to them with other painful experiences that don't make it worthwhile. They really think God is stupid to have created a universe that operates by the so-called "law of attraction." Would God create a system that operated in this manner, regardless of what your heart holds? First of all, the "secret" is not a secret at all. It comes from a verse in the Bible, the New Testament, in the Gospel of Mark (11:24) and I have been using it correctly since I was 13-years-old.

In Mark Chapter 11, verse 24, Jesus states: "Therefore, I say unto you, what things soever ye desire, when ye pray, believe that ye receive them, and ye shall have them."

Another version states it this way:

"Therefore, I tell you, whatever you ask for in prayer, believe that you have received it, and then it will be yours."

The real secret is that The Secret method does not work thoroughly because it ignores a key component. If you study the Bible closely, you will see that Lord Jesus Christ tells His disciples in two verses before this to have FAITH -- and that means without an ounce of doubt in the heart to confess, believe and receive at the same time. This means the mental process of asking, believing and receiving must be done simultaneously NOW. You must ask, believe and receive NOW. It must be locked by faith. You must believe you already have it NOW. Then ACTION comes, because – remember: faith without action is dead. So you receive everything mentally first (the spiritual realm), then you hang on to that steadfastly and through action, you fight to get the physical manifestation. Without one, you can't have the other. Hence:

Faith without action is dead.

Dead is action without faith.

By faith you own what you want in your mind; by action you bring it to fruition.

Some people do the visual work and leave it at that, expecting the law of attraction to bring it to them -- and then they wonder why nothing pans out.

The other important thing to remember is verse 25 of the same chapter of Mark, which states: "And whenever you stand praying, if you have anything against anyone, forgive him/her, that your Father in heaven may also forgive your trespasses."

In other words, cleanse your heart of malice, jealousy, gossip, hatred, deceit and vengeance. You must have a clean heart to receive everything you want blissfully, otherwise you might get what you want with unforgiveness attached to it, which will stop you from enjoying your desired goal.

So now you know that God has designed everything perfectly; and you also know that the creative process is done simultaneously: mentally first, then you must take serious action to bring it to physical realization. You also know that to receive clean blessings, you can't have a heart full of anger, deceit and hatred. You must have a forgiving heart and want the best for everyone; you must truthfully be of service to others with good intentions in order to be fully blessed.

That is exactly why the Bible says, "Fight the good fight of Faith." It means, despite the fact that you have already won mentally (a prerequisite), you must still get out there and fight for what you want and catch up physically to your mental picture. You must "do" it.

Take action. Faith is an action.

You must act on your belief.

Faith is acting on your belief.

F.A.I.T.H. = Follow Action In The Heart

Please pay attention because this is very crucial and the difference between making it and not making it.

Your heart is your subconscious mind -- the seat of all your emotions and beliefs. Once an idea is accepted by your conscious mind and impressed on your subconscious mind, it becomes your belief. Now you take action predicated on the picture (the accepted image as truth) in your mind, your heart, your subconscious mind. Now you must keep fighting the good fight of faith (taking action; acting on your belief) during the gestation period (incubation, growth, development, maturation) until you physically manifest your desired goal. Even the most incredible goals can be attained. You have heard the phrase, "Miracles can come true." They can – if you believe and stay steadfast in your faith.

You always win because you have a victorious picture -- that is your truth and you must keep fighting from your heart and never lose focus in order to bring it to physical fruition. Most importantly, if that picture is drawn on a clean canvas (a pure heart), then everything you receive physically will be yours blissfully. On the contrary, if it is on a dirty canvas (a deceitful heart), you might still get what you want, but with undesired stipulations attached.

Be aware so that you are never caught off-guard. Know where your heart is – and know that you are not using deceit to get what you want. Doing so builds CHARACTER – the topic of our next chapter. Go forth and approach the world with wonder and joy!

Here is an inspiring and salient quote from Albert Einstein: "There are only two ways to live... one is as though nothing is a miracle... the other is as if everything is."

THE 4TH C OF SUCCESS

CHARACTER

The source of all motivation is in your heart.

CHAPTER 4.

CHARACTER

Have you run into some of your old friends from high school or colleagues from your old work place lately? Have you noticed how some of them have not changed a bit? Is it not amazing that they still behave the same way, still tell the same jokes and always reminisce about the past? It seems like they have only developed physically and nothing much else has changed about them. Have you also noticed that they expect you to have stayed the same, too? They still judge everyone according to their past behavior.

Let me give you a simple but poignant example.

I am generally slow at typing and I always hire someone else to type for me. I placed an advertisement for a typist and an old friend Harriet responded. I was excited to go see somebody I already knew.

On the way to see Harriet, I ran into another friend, Bob. I had not seen him for ten years. After exchanging niceties for a few minutes, I told him I was going to see Harriet, an old mutual friend, who had applied for the job. He told me not to go to her and he reminded me how terrible she was at spelling ten years ago.

Of course I did not listen to him because he was judging her according to past behavior and he did not give her the benefit of the doubt that she may have improved. I told Bob that I got good vibes over the phone and I was positive that she was going to do a great job.

I have faith in people and I believe people change, and if someone says they can do something, I simply believe them. I trust my instincts about people.

I went to see Harriet and she was a miracle worker. She typed up my stuff literally as fast as I could speak without one mistake. She had improved tremendously. I thanked her immensely and I have been going to her ever since.

I am glad I listened to my instinct and not somebody else's rumor or gossip or negativity. See, my friend Bob had not changed a bit; he was the same critical, skeptical guy he was ten years ago and because he did not trust people, people did not trust him.

Here is frank advice: let's say you are 40-years-old and your attitude, your way of thinking and your behavior is the same as when you were in your twenties. If this basically describes you, no matter the age, you may need to do some soul searching.

You may have grown physically, but you may not have grown emotionally, mentally and spiritually. It is possible to be physically 40-years-old, but remain spiritually 4-years-old where your spiritual growth is completely untapped and untouched. You have not bothered developing what is by far the most important part of you — your spiritual side. Your spirit is the dimension that in truth constitutes 99% of your genuine existence. IT IS YOUR TRUE SELF.

We are spiritual beings residing in a physical body.

If we are indeed spiritual beings (99%) living in a physical body (1%), how important is it to spend time to get to know and develop our non-physical part? We spend hours pumping iron at the gym and developing our muscles, but remain emotionally and spiritually bankrupt because of lack of knowledge.

It is mind-boggling to think about what the Grand Opulent Designer (GOD), the True Master behind our creation was thinking.

He created all of us equally with the same potential to succeed.

He put unlimited treasure inside our hearts (the spirit) and a little candle. He only gave us one responsibility: to seek, find and light up that candle (through the awareness and acceptance of the

Holy Spirit) so that we could see the treasure and the answer to every problem we confront.

The key to enlightenment, therefore, is inside our hearts, not on the outside. Look inside and light that candle. I believe that is where that word "enlightenment" originated. To enlighten means to shed light upon, to illuminate, to ignite, to kindle. Light up your heart so you can see the treasure in your storehouse.

Become aware of your treasure...

(The Holy Spirit)...

This is the only thing we have to do to develop spiritually.

"Kindle the Candle."

If you are still wondering how you should go about doing this, let us look at the word SPIRIT as an acronym to remind us of a profound message:

S.P.I.R.I.T. = Surrender Peacefully In Receiving Internal Transformation

Transformation occurs when you clean your heart, and let the light come in, which is the topic of the next chapter. Hypothetically speaking, your heart will remain in the dark if you do not light up the candle and you will miss the treasure waiting there. You will take it to the grave unused, untapped, untouched. It is very sad, but true, that a lot of people never get to know the power they possess and the wealth they possess hidden in their own hearts. They leave this world without ever discovering their potential, or excavating their treasure. We all have heard of the expression: "She/He has a heart of gold." It means that person has illuminated the candle and has exposed the gold; and because the treasure is lit up, there is no darkness and that person possesses a cleansed, unadulterated heart.

Character development is essentially spiritual awareness.

In the next chapter, CONDITIONING, I explain the steps to lighting one's heart in detail so that you can approach it methodically without any technical mumbo-jumbo.

THE 5TH C OF SUCCESS

CONDITIONING

Exercise mind and body for an indomitable spirit.

CHAPTER 5.

CONDITIONING

L et me begin this section with this statement I created years ago to help people get into great shape. This is meant to be an all around 4-layer improvement in the enhancement of your life: physically, emotionally, mentally and spiritually.

"Condition your heart to control your body."

"High inner strength is the key to control your body and soul."

You can "Condition your heart" two different ways and one is not independent of the other. I would like to emphasize both because they are equally important.

The first literal meaning of "conditioning" is exercising and keeping your heart in shape so that you can live a long, happy and healthy life. Many people who are extremely busy working on their businesses do not have time for this "petty" activity as I have heard them call it. They claim it is a nuisance to their planned daily activities and they would rather spend the time making money. I am here to tell you that this may be the most important aspect of your success.

What good is it to have all the wealth in the world and not have a healthy body to enjoy it? You cannot possibly continue ignoring this crucial aspect of your life. How many multimillionaires die young because they neglect the importance of exercising and a healthy diet? The good news is that it does not take that much time in a week to keep in shape. It only takes four hours a week: Four different days a week, one hour each designated day where you spend forty minutes of weight training and do twenty minutes of cardiovascular workout, or the other way around. You may also do four hours of your favorite sport: Karate, Basketball, Running, weight training, and so forth.

Note: The above recommended exercise time period is not for professional athletes or those who have competitive aspirations — obviously we all know they need much more.

Despite the fact that our physical bodies constitute 1% of our real existence and our non-physical spirit residing inside our bodies constitutes 99% of our true self, without a healthy body, the spirit cannot thrive.

The spirit cannot reside inside an unhealthy, broken physical vessel. You cannot enjoy your success, accomplishments and riches if you are not healthy.

It is your responsibility to take care of your body and keep it in good shape. We only have this one body and we are accountable for keeping it healthy.

Unfortunately, you cannot go to a supermarket and buy duplicates or spare parts —not yet anyway! You owe it to yourself to exercise your vessel and keep it in good condition so you can enjoy what life has to offer.

When you are happy and vibrant about your physical health and physical shape, you love yourself and you are able to extend that love to others and you feel confident.

The opposite is also true. When you do not exercise, you tend to get lethargic and easily irritated — and as a result of feeling negative emotions, you have low self-esteem.

If you are out of shape and you feel unhealthy, set a goal, make a commitment and use this seven-step-plan to reach your desired goal.

You can do it!

Make it important to your success. Make it part of your daily routine three to four times a week, one hour each session. Discipline yourself with a firm commitment on a consistent basis and do it, regardless of any obstacles.

That covers the first part of conditioning. Now, let us go to the second meaning of "condition your heart."

Condition your heart means cleanse your heart of all negative and self-destructive thoughts, such as- jealousy, anger, gossip, ill-will, hatred, anxiety, revenge, backbiting.

The reason these thoughts and feelings can overtake a person and hold them back from succeeding in their endeavors is often because people have a tendency to compare themselves to others or they compete with others. If somebody else gets a new job or a first place trophy, they often feel like they have been cheated out of an opportunity — as if that trophy was the only one around. Do not worry; there is no lack or shortage in our universe. The universe is limitless and has an endless supply of what you want. There is no need to be jealous of someone else's success. On the contrary, one should be happy for that person so that one may also experience that kind of success.

Two of the most important codes of ethics that we always emphasize at our schools are numbers 19 and 20 which state:

"19: I solemnly pledge to stop competing with others and comparing myself to others.

"20: I solemnly pledge to always want the best for others and be happy for their success."

There are twenty codes of ethics — and the reason we put these two last is because they are two of the hardest to master. Human nature has a tendency to feel jealous of other people's success. Students must understand and embrace these ethics, then put it to practice as they go through four to five years of training (red belt/ black stripe, just before black belt).

Please remember, as I said before: be careful of what you send out with your mind, words and actions.

Whatever you send out, you are sure to get it back multiplied.

This is a universal law and it is inevitable.

The following simple and elementary but poignant diagram says it all. Whatever signal you send out, it is received and matched up by God or the universe and sent back to you multiplied.

What are you sending out?

What are you thinking?

What are you saying?

What are you doing?

BEWARE!!!

BE AWARE!!!

How do you want to live? It is your choice.

Whatever you send out, you are sure to get it back, multiplied.

Choose wisely.

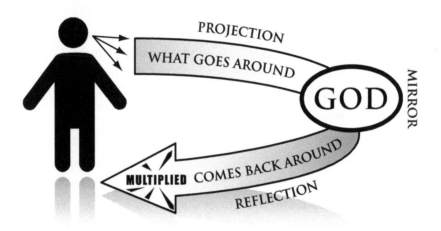

GOD'S UNDENIABLE BOOMERANG

I hope you take the above diagram very seriously. Realize that when you send out a negative signal such as jealousy or ill will toward somebody else, it comes right back to you. Therefore, be careful and do not sabotage your dreams!

Condition your heart so that you may send out good thoughts, such as Love, Peace, Joy, Prosperity, Success, Freedom, Victory, Health, Beauty, Appreciation. When you send these signals out and wish everybody well, you will receive these gifts in return, multiplied!

The Bible in Galatians (5:16-26) states:

"I say then: Walk in the spirit, and you shall not fulfill the lust of the flesh.

"For the flesh lusts against the Spirit, and the Spirit against the flesh; and these are contrary to one another, so that you do not do the things that you wish.

"But if you are led by the Spirit, you are not under the law.

"Now the works of the flesh are evident, which are: adultery, fornication, uncleanness, lewdness,

"idolatry, sorcery, hatred, contentions, jealousies, outbursts of wrath, selfish ambitions, dissensions, heresies,

"envy, murders, drunkenness, revelries, and the like; of which I tell you beforehand, just as I also told you in time past, that those who practice such things will not inherit the Kingdom of God.

"But the fruit of the Spirit is love, joy, peace, longsuffering, kindness, goodness, faithfulness,

"gentleness, self-control. Against such there is no law.

"And those who are Christ's, have crucified the flesh with its passions and desires.

"If we live in the Spirit, let us also walk in the Spirit.

"Let us not become conceited, provoking one another, envying one another."

THE 6TH C OF SUCCESS

CONCENTRATION

Play to win: focus on your target. Never quit.

CHAPTER 6.

CONCENTRATION

Concentration is the ability to direct your focused energy to a single objective. It is putting your attention on your intention.

Concentrate on your objective incessantly!

Do not get distracted or deviated from your main course, regardless of any temptations.

Take a look at the list of actions you have jotted down for you to take on a daily basis (no matter how small). Break everything down into smaller individual tasks and take action. Resolve to do something every single day that will move you toward your major goal. This will keep your focus and attention on where you are going.

What do you think about throughout the day?

What is your concentration about?

What do you dream about daily?

Do you only think about your goal every now and then and put it away for the future and expect to receive something? I hope the answer to this question is not affirmative because it will not work that way.

You need to set aside at least ten minutes a day in a quiet and peaceful place to deliberately meditate (pray), focus and concentrate on your desired goals.

Make that your dominant thought.

Remember, your dominant thought becomes your belief and that belief becomes your truth and ultimately it manifests physically in your outside world through your actions.

When you pray or meditate, close your eyes and see in your mind's eye the image of the victorious outcome of your goal and see yourself in the possession of the desired goal, revel in it and be grateful.

Now that your mental work is done and you believe you have received it and you own it by faith in the spirit realm, then take action on your belief to catch up with that image and make it physical.

Hold on to that triumphant image with unshakable faith unceasingly — and take action n.o.w.

Faith is N.O.W.

"No Obstacles Whatsoever!"

Imagine thinking that there is no obstacle whatsoever for any desired goal you may have. You develop a positive and limitless attitude towards everything you want.

Regardless of what is going on, if you keep your positive mental attitude, you will automatically be driven toward your goal.

But remember, you have to act. You have to "do."

You must take action.

Concentration is key to success. You can get amazing results by focusing on your intention; however, if you are sporadic and dispersed, do not expect to see clear and concrete results.

The best time I choose to instill new ideas, concepts or a new way of thinking into my students' minds is after a tremendously exhilarating workout. They are in the most receptive mode because their thoughts are focused, their minds are quiet and their attitudes are humble. Their resistance to new ideas is low and their guards are down while their hearts and minds are wide open for new impressions.

Whereas, if I tried to do the same without a hard workout, their resistance would be very high and their guards would be up; they would not be as receptive to new ideas. Their EGOs would get in the way and they would question everything.

To me, a memorable acronym for E.G.O. is **E**dging **G**od **O**ut.

I would recommend concentrating after a vigorous workout. A hearty physical workout is a wonderful prelude to visualizing and meditating on your dreams.

Concentrate on the things that you want, not on the things you do not want. Many people unconsciously think about the things they do not want and they get surprised when they get the very thing they did not want. Whether you want it or not, the fact that you are thinking it and saying it, you are going to get it because your actions will be driven to match your predominant thought.

You always get what you want and what you do not want; it all depends on which one you focus on; so, focus only on what you want.

Allow no other possibility!

Allow me to elaborate on this because it is extremely important for you to know how the mind works. If you say, for instance, "I don't want to get sick," you will surely get sick because you are still talking and thinking about sickness. The harder you try to push that away from you, the easier it will come to you. Force negates, therefore, whatever you try to resist, it will surely persist because you are giving it your focus and attention unconsciously!

If you don't want to get sick, then focus on staying healthy. Don't allow yourself to slide into thinking the negative possibility.

You get more of what you focus on, negative or positive.

Change your thoughts now and change your future.

The Bible in Philippians (4:8) tells us what to concentrate on:

"...whatever things are true, whatever things are noble, whatever things are just, whatever things are pure, whatever things are lovely, whatever things are of good report, if there is any virtue and if there is anything praiseworthy — meditate on these things."

THE 7TH C OF SUCCESS

CONTRIBUTION

Your greatest gift is sharing your talents.

CHAPTER 7.

CONTRIBUTION

The last but not least element of success is Contribution. To contribute means to give of yourself to others in the form of time, knowledge, assistance and material support.

I established Shaun T Benjamin Karate academy in Glendale, California, to primarily help others discover their power within and their unlimited potential for success through the practice of a transformational Martial Arts program: H.I.G.H. K.E.Y. F.I.T.N.E.S.S. The acronyms stand for:

Honesty, Integrity, Generosity, Humility, Kindness, Excellence, Yearning, Faith, Invincibility, Tenacity, Nobility, Equality, Self-Control, S.P.I.R.I.T.

I spent a lot of years carefully creating and designing this transformational program in order to take the students through a journey of self-discovery. This amazing transformational program through the use of Martial Arts will be discussed in detail in my next book. HIGH KEY FITNESS: TAP IN AND WIPE OUT YOUR VICES.

There is a list of twenty codes of ethics that was created to utilize at different stages to teach our students to enhance their lives. Through this transformational journey, students become aware of their internal strength and how much they can contribute to society at large. They learn that their main purpose in life is to fulfill their greatest potential at whatever they pursue and, in turn, contribute to other people's lives by being fully realized spiritual beings.

Our Code of ethics number 16 states:

"16. I solemnly pledge to be a giver in life because it is by giving that I receive."

It is the same as the universal law of sowing and reaping.

You reap what you sow.

We each have a special gift from God within us. We are supposed to find what that gift is and develop it, get good at it and then contribute to others.

Years ago, I used to work for Boeing as an aerospace engineering manager assigned to the center fuselage on the C-17 cargo plane. I will never forget what one of my colleagues, Dr. J., a brilliant man, said to me: "Shaun, when the end of your life comes and you face God for judgment, He will only ask you one question: 'Steward, what have you done with the gifts I gave you?'"

With each gift there is a responsibility to share it with other people and contribute to their lives in a positive manner. I will never forget what Dr. J said to me on that day. It made a tremendous impact on my life. I suddenly realized that I had been blessed with many gifts that I was not utilizing to help others.

I have since created the "H.I.G.H. K.E.Y. F.I.T.N.E.S.S." sport karate system, which is an international curriculum for transformation through the use of the Martial Arts and have been teaching it in our facility in Glendale, CA. It essentially teaches that karate is for self-improvement and self-discovery rather than only self-defense. It's Soul-Defense. It teaches the students to find their gifts and operate at their God-given potential to contribute. I have also written a screenplay called *A Fighting Chance* that is based on my philosophy and creation of High Key Fitness.

A Fighting Chance is a family action sports drama that will be produced by my production company, Melody Films Entertainment, Inc., which was created to produce life-affirming, inspirational and uplifting movies and television shows to promote moral values. www.MelodyFilmsEntertainment.com

I have also created *Nothing But the Truth Acting* system (Divine8Acting), an international acting curriculum that teaches the creation of truth and nothing but the truth through the spirit. It is designed for anyone around the world with a desire to become a great actor/actress.

I am currently in the process of writing a screenplay, *Acting Crazy*, based on my acting philosophy and the complex Hollywood system. It is a family drama about believing in one's dreams and overcoming obstacles.

In sum, I am pursuing my dreams and goals by exerting positive action: imagining, professing, creating, C'ing, doing!

It is important for you to search and discover your hidden talents, too, so that you may contribute to others in a positive manner. My instructors and I always remind our students to have an "attitude of gratitude" with the gifts they have been given and to have an appreciation and admiration for other people's gifts for their contribution. Be thankful for everything you have because when you are grateful for what you have, you get more of it!

If you are learning a new skill and the instructor asks for her/his hourly rate, pay it gladly and bless them with it. When you do that, you get blessed too, and you will continue to prosper. However, if you give grudgingly, you get nothing back. Therefore, give generously and cheerfully, because you are sending that signal out — and guess what? You get more of it back! I live this and see this principle in action all the time.

I have to take a minute here to say how grateful I am to have been blessed with a beautiful wife, Vera, who has been my rock solid support and has given me the most amazing gifts of my life: my son Mike (Vrej) and my daughter Melo (Melody). I am grateful to God for our children who have taught me how to love, to give and to be kind and not judgmental. I am also grateful for my brother and sisters who constantly give generously to others and never ask for anything back. I am eternally indebted to them for enriching my life. This is what contribution is all about – giving selflessly to others.

Do not live in a cocoon. Contribute to other people's lives by sharing your knowledge, inventions, creations, and solutions. Imagine if Edison or Graham Bell or Einstein did not share their discoveries!

Imagine if our great country did not share its' computer technology with the rest of the world, where would we all be? One of the main reasons the United States is so prosperous and blessed as a nation is because she is extremely generous and contributes to the rest of the world financially and technologically. The United States is typically first to respond with humanitarian aid when there are disasters in foreign lands. It is no wonder we are a land of freedom, prosperity and opportunity.

When you contribute to another person's life, you contribute to humanity. Whether you contribute one-on-one or to millions of people, by touching one life and making a difference, you have affected the very fabric of mankind. No positive action or deed is too small or too large. They all contribute when you contribute!

The fact of the matter is that every truly successful, caring person has a noble objective that is intended for the benefit of mankind. Realizing and acting on that good intention is true success!

CONCLUSION

Now that we are aware of the significance and the power of our uttered words, projected thoughts and actions, we should be cautious about what we think about all day long. Since we create our own future by what we project NOW, we should carefully and mindfully make wise choices that would benefit us.

Only you can stop yourself from reaching your goal by giving power to fear, anxiety, worry and other negative emotions.

Fear is a paralyzer, whereas Faith is a mobilizer.

With Faith, all things are possible.

F.A.I.T.H. = **F**ollow **A**ction **I**n **T**he **H**eart

In other words: act on what you believe.

Take action!

Do what your heart tells you to do.

That is your inner intuition tugging at the strings of your heart, telling you it is time for you to take action. That type of action is guaranteed to bring you your desired results.

Never give up on your goal!

Never quit!

Be clear about where you are going and know that you will get there with confidence.

Do not hope, wish, guess or vacillate.

In my created acronym list, HOPE stands for:

H.O.P.E.= **H**allucinating **O**n **P**lanet **E**arth

Wishful thinking or hopeful thinking will not give you concrete results and will not get you to your final destination. You have to go beyond hope; you have to believe, trust, have faith – and act upon your goals!

There is an old saying I picked up a long time ago from my mother that I have carried with me for the last twenty years. It is an Old English proverb, passed down for generations:

Fear knocked at the door.

Faith answered.

No one was there.

Once you follow the 7 C's, you should release all your desires to God. Place your Confidence in God for the ultimate return. Trust that He will fulfill your desires (He will fill your dream and send it back to you full) only if you act on your belief. Use the 7 C's to bring yourself closer to the Big C – The Creator. God Almighty. With Him as your partner, it is impossible to fail. With Him on your side, you always win!

I finish here by saying what we tell our students:

Be grateful for everything.

Have faith and have fun.

Be good; do good.

Know that God is with you always if you acknowledge Him.

May you all reach your dreams.

Know that you can and you will.

We love you all.

God bless you all!

And I will leave you with this last summation by my son's character in my screenplay "A Fighting Chance." at the end of the movie.

"I am now convinced, through my Dad's teachings, that there is a higher power in the universe that loves us, watches over us and grants us our wishes, only if we turn to it and acknowledge it, with a loving heart, a humble attitude and an unshakable FAITH."

Melody Films Entertainment, Inc.
Shaun T Benjamin Karate
730 S. Central Ave. # 111
Glendale, CA 91204
818-331-0049
818-583-0049
ShaunTBenjamin@gmail.com
Shauntbejanian@gmail.com

BIBLICAL PASSAGES for the 7 C's

(DAILY AFFIRMATIONS)

Use these motivational messages and words of inspiration to help remind you and guide you through the processes toward success!

1. COMMITMENT

"Commit to the Lord whatever you do, and He will establish your plans."

— Proverbs 16:3

Daily Affirmation:

I am committed to creation, not destruction; I am committed to love, not hatred; I am committed to courage, not fear; I am committed to faith, not vacillation; I am committed to joy and all things positive for my life and others'. I cast out despair, negative thoughts and gloom. I am committed to my desired goal and I pledge to stay faithful until its fruition.

2. CONSISTENCY

"All Scripture is breathed out by God and profitable for teaching, for reproof, for correction, and for training in righteousness."

— 2 Timothy 3:16

"Forgetting what is behind and straining toward what is ahead,

I press on toward the goal to win the prize for which God has called me heavenward in Christ Jesus."

— Philippians 3:13-14

Daily Affirmation:

I act upon my dreams and I move forward, no matter the obstacles, to come closer to my goal. I am disciplined and I take action daily no matter what.

3. CONFIDENCE

"For the Lord shall be thy Confidence, and shall keep thy foot from being taken."

— Proverbs 3:26

"But blessed are those who trust in the Lord and have made the Lord their hope and confidence."

— Jeremiah 17:7

Daily Affirmation:

I cannot be stopped because I am cloaked in the confidence of my faith, which makes me stronger the more someone tries to undo my efforts. I have the conviction of the spirit and the power of God working on my side for me to attain and fulfill my goal. I know where I am going and I believe I will get there because I act on my belief through F.A.I.T.H. N.O.W. = **F**ollow **A**ction **I**n **T**he **H**eart, **N**o **O**bstacles **W**hatsoever.

4. CHARACTER

"Kings take pleasure in honest lips; they value persons who speak what is right."

— Proverbs 16:13

"Let no corrupting talk come out of your mouths, but only such as is good for building up, as fits the occasion, that it may give grace to those who hear."
— Ephesians 4:29

Daily Affirmation

I am a person of integrity because I listen to my spirit, my heart — and it guides me because it is the voice of God. I know right from wrong; and I know that doing what is right is not the easiest path to take. But in the end, it is the right path to take because being true and honest to my inner self gives me the power to know I am leading my life with God at my side and I grow spiritually.

5. CONDITIONING

"Above all else, guard your heart, for it is the wellspring of life."
— Proverbs 4:23

"Do you not know that your body is a temple of the Holy Spirit, who is in you, whom you have received from God? You are not your own; you were bought at a price. Therefore honor God with your body."
— 1 Corinthians 6:19-20

Daily Affirmation

My heart is open and pure and that is why my commitment is unwavering. I will keep a healthy heart — both physically and spiritually — because I want to enjoy all that God has made. It is my duty to God and my own body to think of my vessel as the home to God's grace. I know that the more goodness I send out into the world, I will receive it back amplified in many ways — and I will be forever fueled to be a loving and gracious person with compassion.

6. CONCENTRATION

"Finally, brothers/sisters, whatever is true, whatever is noble, whatever is right, whatever is pure, whatever is lovely, whatever is admirable—if anything is excellent or praiseworthy — think about such things."
— Philippians 4:8

Daily Affirmation

I concentrate on my goal and focus on the positive; I never waiver. I will not exhaust any energy by giving negative thoughts a chance; I will destroy the negative thoughts with my keen focus on all that is good and all that I need to do to accomplish my dreams and aspirations. God helps me to think about truth, honesty, purity. My thoughts are powerful because they are positive and focused. My concentration undoes the impossible.

7. CONTRIBUTION

"In everything I did, I showed you that by this kind of hard work we must help the weak, remembering the words the Lord Jesus Himself said: 'It is more blessed to give than to receive.'"
— Acts 20:35

"Give, and it will be given to you. They will pour into your lap a good measure — pressed down, shaken together, and running over. For by your standard of measure it will be measured to you in return."
— Luke 6:38

Daily Affirmation

It is God's will that I attain my dreams so that I may share my ultimate gifts with others. I am constantly receiving gifts and blessings because I am a giving person.